I0004949

Book 1
Excel Shortcuts

BY SAM KEY

&

Book 2
CSS Programming Professional Made Easy

BY SAM KEY

Book 1

Excel Shortcuts

BY SAM KEY

The 100 Top Best Powerful Excel Keyboard Shortcuts in 1 Day!

Programming Box Set #73: Excel Shortcuts & CSS Programming Professional Made Easy

Programming Box Set #73: Excel Shortcuts & CSS Programming Professional Made Easy

Table Of Contents

Introduction

I want to thank you and congratulate you for purchasing the book, "The Power of Excel Shortcuts: The 100 Top Best Powerful Excel Keyboard Shortcuts in 1 Day!".

This book contains proven steps and strategies on how to master the Microsoft Excel through just 100 keyboard shortcuts! However, most people will ask, "Why do you need to learn these shortcuts anyway?"

Advantages of Using Microsoft Excel

Microsoft Excel has become one of the most commonly used enterprise software in schools and offices. Its way of presenting data, which is through a spreadsheet, has helped a lot of people especially in the field of data mining. If you were going to put numerous rows of data, in let's say, a word processing program, it might take a lot of time creating tables and formatting each of them to fit in the pages. With the Microsoft Excel, these manual tasks are now much easier.

What does the Microsoft Excel have that other programs don't? For one, it has a built-in spreadsheet that you can manipulate the size and formatting. This versatile way of maneuvering the spreadsheet made it indispensable for many. Now, gone are the days were people have to manually draw tables in sheets of paper. Excel has already the tables prepared for them.

Another nifty feature of this software is its calculation function. Excel houses a myriad of formulas for solving arithmetic, financial and logical problems, among others. Thus, one doesn't even need to calculate every sum or average of a data series. Just by using a formula in Excel, everything can be done in an instant.

The Secret behind Mastering Excel

Speaking of instant, did you know that Excel has more than a hundred keyboard shortcuts? What does this mean to you as an Excel user? It means you can continuously work on your Excel spreadsheet without having to depend on your mouse constantly for Excel functions.

This is especially helpful whenever you are inputting a lot of data, and doing this will be more efficient if both of your hands weren't switching from keyboard to mouse and vice versa, every once in a while. In addition, if your mouse suddenly chose the most inopportune time to malfunction, learning Excel shortcuts can save you from major headaches.

As such, this book will provide you 100 keyboard shortcuts which you can use in Excel. In addition, as a bonus, you will learn about alternatives in case you forget any of these shortcuts.

Thanks again for purchasing this book, I hope you enjoy it!

Chapter 1: Moving Around the Excel Screen

People typically use the mouse for navigating the Excel screen. With this device, you can manipulate every cell in Excel, including its formatting and color. Since the mouse can access the major functions in Excel through the ribbon, there is no need for you to manually-type every formula or command.

However, the only difficult thing that you cannot do with a mouse is entering text. If you're going to use an on-screen keyboard, keying in the data in every cell would probably take you a lot longer than just using the keyboard for the text.

Thus, if you're going to use the keyboard most of the time, especially if you're just starting to build the spreadsheet data from scratch, it would be helpful to learn the basic keyboard shortcuts for moving around the Excel spreadsheet.

Shortcut #1: Arrow Keys

There are four arrow keys found in the right side of your main keyboard keys. These are the Arrow Left, Arrow Right, Arrow Up, and Arrow Down keys. Intuitively, you know that you can use these keys for moving within the spreadsheet. For instance, by selecting a cell then pressing Arrow Up, it will situate the cursor in the cell directly above your selected cell.

Shortcut #2: Ctrl + Arrow Key

Let's assume that you have a block of Excel data that spans more than 50,000 rows and more than 200 columns. You would probably have a hard time using a mouse in skimming these voluminous data. As such, you can use the Ctrl + Arrow key to navigate each "ends" of the data easily. In this example, click any cell in the block of data then press Ctrl + Arrow Down. You will be immediately located to the bottom cell in that specific column.

Shortcut #3: Shift + Arrow Key

You have selected all the items in the row but you forgot to include one cell. What would you do if you needed to include the next cell in the selection? Simply press Shift + Arrow Key, where the arrow pertains to the direction of the region you want to highlight.

Shortcut #4: Ctrl + Shift + Arrow Key

The above shortcut only includes one cell in the selection; but what would happen if you want to include everything until the last cell containing a data? You then use the Ctrl + Shift + Arrow Key.

Shortcut #5: Backspace

The Backspace key immediately deletes the contents of the active cell. However, if the cell is in Edit mode, it will only delete one character in the left of the insertion point, or the blinking cursor in the Formula bar.

Shortcut #6: Delete

This key has the same function as the Backspace key. However, instead of the left side, it removes a character in the right hand side of the insertion point.

Shortcut #7: End

Pressing the End key will enable the End Mode in Excel. In this mode, if you press an Arrow key, it will directly take you to the last used cell (or if none, last cell) in that specific direction. However, if the Scroll Lock is on, pressing the End key will only take you to the lower right corner of your Excel screen.

Shortcut #8: Ctrl + End

It works the same as the End key where pressing this combination will take you to the last used cell. However, if no cells were used, it will not move to the end of the worksheet like the End key does. Also, if the insertion point is located in the Formula bar (e.g., after the first character), Ctrl + End will put this cursor at the end of the field.

Shortcut #9: Ctrl + Shift + End

This keyboard shortcut can do two functions. First, in the Formula bar, it will select every character at the right of the insertion point. On the other hand, if you use it in the worksheet, it will highlight the cells starting from the active cell (or selected cell) until the last used cell in the worksheet.

Shortcut #10: Spacebar

Aside from putting a space in your text, it can also either select or clear a checkbox.

Shortcut #11: Ctrl + Spacebar

This will select the whole column to where the active cell is located.

Shortcut #12: Shift + Spacebar

It has the same function as the above, but this shortcut selects rows instead of columns.

Shortcut #13: Ctrl + Shift + Spacebar

Pressing these keys will select your entire worksheet.

Shortcut #14: Enter

After you have entered a data in a cell, pressing the Enter key will complete the input of data. Besides that, you can also directly go one cell below through this key. Considered as the most commonly used shortcut in Excel, you will be using the Enter key quite a lot because all Excel functions need it.

Shortcut #15: Shift + Enter

If you press Enter, you will go down one cell. Conversely, a Shift + Enter will complete an entry in a cell but the cursor will go directly above your entry.

Shortcut #16: Ctrl + Enter

Since this is a spreadsheet, it follows that after you have put an entry, you will enter another data below it. That is the common task whenever you're working on a table or database, which explains why the Enter key goes down. However, if you think that you need the downward movement, you can try Ctrl + Enter. This will plainly enter your data in the cell and it won't move your cursor to another direction.

Shortcut #17: Alt + Enter

You want the data to go into the next line in the same cell. However, if you press Enter, the cursor just moves on to the next cell in line. Pressing the Tab key doesn't work either. So what will you do? Try Alt + Enter key and see if it works.

Shortcut #18: Esc Key

The Escape key, or simply "Esc", performs a lot of nifty functions in Excel. Among of which are the following: 1) deletes a whole data in a cell, 2) exits you from a dialog box, and 3) escapes you from the full screen mode of Excel.

Shortcut #19: Home Key

The Home key will take you to the first cell in the specific row of your active cell. However, if the Scroll Lock is on, the cursor will go to the upper-left corner of your current window.

Shortcut #20: Ctrl + Home

This shortcut, also known as the "True Home key", brings the user to the beginning of the worksheet.

Shortcut #21: Ctrl + Shift + Home

This will select all cells from the active cell up to the first cell in the worksheet.

Shortcut #22: Page Down

Scouring among rows and rows of worksheets is now easy because of this button. This will display the next page in your Excel window.

Shortcut #23: Alt + Page Down

Unlike Page Down, the Alt + Page Down combination will show the next page to the right of your current window.

Shortcut #24: Ctrl + Page Down

Flipping in several worksheets is now easy thanks to Ctrl + Page Down. This will automatically turn you over to the next worksheet.

Shortcut #25: Ctrl + Shift + Page Down

The normal way of selecting several worksheets at once is to hold Ctrl while clicking each of the worksheets to be included in the selection.

However, for those who don't think this is the practical way to do it, here's an alternative. Use the Ctrl + Shift + Page Down; it will automatically select the sheets for you.

Shortcut #26: Page Up

This is quite similar to Shortcut #22: Page Down key, except for the fact that this one goes in the opposite direction (which is upward).

Shortcut #27: Alt + Page Up

The Alt + Page Up will move your screen to the left, instead of right as what was described in Shortcut #23: Alt + Page Down.

Shortcut #28: Ctrl + Page Up

Same as Shortcut #24: Ctrl + Page Down, this will enable you to change sheets easily. However, this one goes in a counterclockwise direction.

Shortcut #29: Ctrl + Shift + Page Up

Selecting sheets is also a function of the Ctrl + Shift + Page Up. However, it will select the worksheets on the left hand side of your current sheet first.

Shortcut #30: Tab Key

Using the Tab key will enable you to move to the right hand side of the cell. Also, if you have a protected worksheet, pressing this can immediately take you to the next unlocked cell. Lastly, in case there is a dialog box, you can easily move along the options through the Tab key.

Shortcut #31: Shift + Tab

The Shift + Tab works the opposite way; if pressing Tab will take you to the right hand cell, this shortcut will locate the left cell for you. It also applies to the other functions of the Tab key. In a dialog box for instance, keying in Shift + Tab will move you to the previous option.

Shortcut #32: Ctrl + Tab

You're now done with shortcuts for moving around cells and worksheets. As such, the succeeding shortcuts in this chapter will focus on dialog boxes. For this shortcut, use it if you want to go to the next tab in a dialog box.

Shortcut #33: Ctrl + Shift + Tab

However, if you wish to go back to the previous tab in a dialog box, using the Ctrl + Shift + Tab is the right combination.

So there you have it, the first 33 keyboard shortcuts in Excel. Hopefully, through these tips you can know traverse in your multitude of cells and worksheets with no difficulty at all.

Chapter 2: Navigating the Excel Ribbon

Microsoft created the "ribbon" as a replacement to the expanding menus in the earlier versions of Microsoft Excel. It houses all the functions in Excel such as formatting, page layout, pictures, and shapes. However, since its interface is not in an expanding menu style, people are not that familiar with its keyboard shortcuts as compared to before where you can immediately see which shortcut runs which.

To help you with that, here are some of the most commonly used keyboard shortcuts for exploring the Ribbon.

Shortcut #34: Alt Key

Letters and numbers will appear in the ribbon once you push the Alt key. What happens is that it activates the access keys, wherein typing in corresponding letter or number will let you select a specific function in the ribbon.

Shortcut #35: F10

This key has the same function as the Alt key, only that pressing the F10 would require you to use your right hand instead.

Shortcut #36: Alt + Arrow Left/Right

To be able to navigate to the other tabs, use these keys.

Shortcut #37: F10 + Arrow Left/Right

Since it was previously mentioned that the F10 behaves the same way as the Alt key, pressing F10 followed by an arrow to the left or to the right will also transfer you to other tabs.

Shortcut #38: Ctrl + F1

There's no doubt that the ribbon indeed takes up quite a lot of space in your screen. Therefore, for those who want more area for their spreadsheet, hiding the ribbon is the best option. To do that, simply press Ctrl + F1. To show the ribbon again, also press the same shortcut.

Shortcut #39: Shift + F10

Shift + F10 is similar to the right click button of your mouse. It can open menus and other options depending on where your cursor is.

Shortcut #40: F6

You can move along three areas of the screen through this key. The F6 key, will take you either to the ribbon, the spreadsheet, or the status bar.

Shortcut #41: F10 + Tab

In a tab, you can browse through the functions by pressing this combination continuously. You can also press this shortcut first, and then proceed with the arrow keys for navigation.

Shortcut #42: F10 + Shift + Tab

The above shortcut goes around the functions in a clockwise manner. On the contrary, the F10 + Shift + Tab shortcut does otherwise.

Shortcut #43: F1

In the upper right corner of the ribbon, there is a blue question mark icon. Accessing this icon will take you to the Microsoft Excel Help task pane. Alternatively, if you press F1 the same pane will open.

Since the area around the ribbon is limited, it is only appropriate that there would be less keyboard shortcuts dedicated for it. All in all, there are ten button combinations for the ribbon.

Chapter 3: Formatting the Excel Spreadsheet

If you're also a user of the Microsoft Word, you are probably familiar with formatting keyboard shortcuts such as Ctrl + B, which stands for bold text or Ctrl + I, which italicizes your text. Since you can do almost every basic feature that you need in the Word application through the keyboard, this makes the formatting easier for you.

Fortunately, even though Excel is not a word-processing program, it also has dedicated keyboard shortcuts that for formatting. These are as follows:

Shortcut #44: Alt + '

By going to the Styles group in the Home tab, you can quickly change the appearance of the cell by selecting any of the pre-installed styles in Excel. To see the formatting changes done within a cell, you click on the New Style option, which will take you to the Style dialog box. Similarly, clicking Alt + ' will get you in the same menu.

Shortcut #45: Ctrl + B

Like in Microsoft Word, Ctrl + B will either apply or remove a bold format in a text.

Shortcut #46: Ctrl + 2

This shortcut can also make the selected text into a bold type.

Shortcut #47: Ctrl + I

Letter I stands for Italics. As such, clicking Ctrl + I will turn any text into an italicized type.

Shortcut #48: Ctrl + 3

This also functions like the Ctrl + I shortcut.

Shortcut #49: Ctrl + U

Ctrl + U will put an underline in the selected text.

Shortcut #50: Ctrl + 4

Another alternative for the Ctrl +U is the Ctrl + 4 shortcut.

Shortcut #51: Ctrl + 5

To easily put a strikethrough in your text, press Ctrl + 5.

Shortcut #52: Ctrl + Shift + F

If you want more font formatting options, you can just proceed to the Font tab of the Format cells dialog box. Right-clicking a cell then selecting Format Cells will get you there, or you can just use this shortcut.

Shortcut #53: Ctrl + Shift + P

This shortcut works the same as the above.

Shortcut #54: Ctrl + Shift + &

Now that you're done with editing the text, this shortcut as well as the succeeding ones will pertain to cell formatting. As for Ctrl + Shift + &, it will put a plain black border on all sides of the cell.

Shortcut #55: Ctrl + Shift + _

On the contrary, Ctrl + Shift + _ will remove the borders that you have made.

Shortcut #56: F4

Instead of manually doing all the formatting for a number of cells, Excel has a shortcut wherein you can redo the formatting that you just did in another cell. This is the F4 function key. For example, if you have put borders in Cell A1, selecting Cell A2 then pressing F4 will also create borders for that specific cell.

Shortcut #57: Ctrl + 1

Pressing the Ctrl + 1 will show the Format Cells dialog box. In this box, you can edit every possible formatting for a cell such as number format, alignment, font, border, and fill.

The previous chapters have discussed how certain shortcuts can perform specific functions in Excel such as formatting cells and navigating the spreadsheet. In the following chapters, the topics will be about the different uses of specific buttons such as the Function keys and the Control key.

Chapter 4: Working with Function Keys

The first row of keys in your keyboard contains the function keys, which is denoted by the letter F followed by a number. In the Windows desktop, these function keys can do a variety of tasks such as adjusting the screen brightness or minimizing the volume.

Excel uses the function keys for different purposes. Thus, most people usually have a difficulty mastering the Function key shortcuts in Excel.

Shortcut #58: Alt + F1

Alt + F1 will automatically create a chart for you. Just select the range of cells containing your chart data then press this shortcut. Afterwards, a column chart will appear in the worksheet.

Shortcut #59: Alt + Shift + F1

The normal way in creating a new worksheet is by right-clicking any of the existing worksheets then choosing Insert. The same task can be done by this shortcut.

Shortcut #60: F2

In editing a formula, you can't just simply select an active cell; you have to click on the Formula bar so that you can make changes to it. Fortunately, the F2 will put the cell in Edit mode. Thus, if you want to amend a cell, there's no need for you to click on the Formula bar; just use F2 instead.

Shortcut #61: Shift + F2

The Shift + F2 shortcut will insert comments in the active cell.

Shortcut #62: Ctrl + F2

Unlike the previous F2 combinations, this one has nothing to do with editing a cell. When you press Ctrl + F2, you will be forwarded to the Print Preview screen. Upon exiting this screen, your spreadsheet will show dotted lines which serves as a marker for a page border.

Shortcut #63: F3

Instead of constantly referring to a range of cells by their cell location (e.g., A1:D1), you can just define a name for this range. Thus, whenever you want to pertain to that specific range in a formula, you can simply put its name; there's no need for you to put the cell range. F3 will take you to the Paste Name dialog box, wherein you can list all the names created in a worksheet and their respective cell references.

Shortcut #64: Ctrl + F3

To create a new name, go to the Name Manager through Ctrl + F3.

Shortcut #65: Shift + F3

Using formulas is the heart of Microsoft Excel. Without it, you cannot do any calculations in the spreadsheet. As such, there is a dedicated tab for Formulas in the Excel ribbon. However, it may take quite a lot of time for users to efficiently look for the appropriate formula with all the possible options in the Formulas tab. Because of this, the Shift + F3 key combination is made. It opens the Insert Function dialog box, wherein you can easily search for a formula by just typing in the description of what you need to do.

Shortcut #66: Ctrl + F4

You don't need to click that "X" mark in the upper left corner of your Excel screen just to close the application; a simple Ctrl + F4 is enough to do the job.

Shortcut #67: F5

Rummaging through a lot of cells takes a lot of work, especially if you're dealing with thousands of rows in a spreadsheet. The Go To dialog box, which can be accessed through F5, will help you reach that specific cell or range that you wanted to see.

Shortcut #68: Ctrl + F5

By default, all workbooks are always in full screen mode in Excel. However, if you're doing work on several Excel files at once, it may be hard to switch from one file to the other when each workbook is on full screen. Through Ctrl + F5, the selected file restore to window size in the Excel screen so that you can easily switch across files.

Shortcut #69: Shift + F6

This works the same as Shortcut #40: F6, albeit in a counterclockwise direction.

Shortcut #70: Ctrl + F6

If you have more than one workbook open, pressing Ctrl + F6 will let you switch among these workbooks.

Shortcut #71: F7

Aside from Microsoft Word, the Excel application has also a built-in spell checker. To check the spelling of every word in your spreadsheet, press F7. This will run the Spelling dialog box. Apart from detecting erroneous spellings, it also suggests possible words that can replace the incorrect word.

Shortcut #72: Ctrl + F7

As mentioned before, you should not use the full screen mode when working with several Excel files. This is so that you can select each workbook with ease. The Ctrl + F7 shortcut executes the Move command so that you can drag the unneeded workbooks in another area in the Excel screen where it can't obstruct your view.

Shortcut #73: F8

Upon pressing F8, the Excel goes into an Extend Selection mode. This enables you to use the arrow keys to extend the current selection. Pressing the same key will also lift the Extend Selection mode.

Shortcut #74: Shift + F8

The limitation of the F8 key is that it only adds adjacent cells in the selection. Through Shift + F8, you can now add any nonadjacent cell by using arrow keys.

Shortcut #75: Ctrl + F8

To resize your workbook, use Ctrl + F8. This will run the Size command for workbooks that are not in a full screen mode.

Shortcut #76: Alt + F8

A macro is a set of actions created using the Visual Basic programming language. What it does is to automate a set of tasks in Excel. For example, you're going to retrieve a data in a one sheet then you'll paste the said data in another sheet. However, if you're going to do the copy-paste task for thousands of data, it might take you a long time. As such, you can use the macro for this. Alt + F8 will open the Macro dialog box, where you can record and run a macro.

Shortcut #77: F9

This is the Refresh button in Excel. Once you refresh a workbook, it will recalculate all new formulas in the said file.

Shortcut #78: Shift + F9

On the other hand, Shift + F9 will only recalculate the formulas in the worksheet you are currently working on.

Shortcut #79: Ctrl + Alt + F9

This has the same function as F9, but it will also recalculate formulas that have not been changed.

Shortcut #80: Ctrl + Alt + Shift + F9

Aside from doing what the Ctrl + Alt + F9 shortcut does, it also rechecks all dependent formulas for any errors.

Shortcut #81: Alt + Shift + F10

Smart tags are data that are labeled in a particular type. For instance, a person's name in an Outlook email message can be labeled with this tag. You can open the smart tag menu through this shortcut.

Shortcut #82: Ctrl + F10

This will enable a workbook to display in full screen mode (or maximized mode).

Shortcut #83: F11

The Shortcut #58: Alt + F1 will let you create charts by highlighting the data series. Similarly, the F11 key has the same function except that you don't need to select the data series; it will automatically detect the data for you. Another difference between these two shortcuts is that the Alt + F1 will display the chart in the same worksheet, while the F1 key will make another worksheet for the new chart.

Shortcut #84: Shift + F11

This is an alternative to Shortcut #59: Alt + Shift + F1, wherein it will insert a new worksheet.

Shortcut #85: Alt + F11

Alt + F11 will open the Microsoft Visual Basic Editor. In this menu, you can create or edit a macro by using the Visual Basic for Applications (VBA) programming language.

Shortcut #86: F12

The F12 key is the shortcut for the Save As dialog box. It lets you save your Excel file among the available formats.

In case you're wondering why the F1, F4, F6 and F10 keys as well as some of their derivatives are not included in the list, these function keys have already been discussed in the previous chapters. Moreover, as this book specifically claims that it will contain at least a hundred keyboard shortcuts, putting these function keys again in the list will not create an accurate count of all the shortcuts.

Chapter 5: Discovering Ctrl Combinations

There are more than 50 Ctrl key combinations that you can use in the Excel sheet, with some shortcuts comprising of special characters instead of the usual alphanumeric ones. Thus, it would be unpractical to include every possible shortcut, especially if there's a little chance that a typical user will use them all.

With these reasons, only the f14 most valuable Ctrl shortcuts will be contained in the list below.

Shortcut #87: Ctrl + ;

Ctrl + ; will show the current date in the active cell.

Shortcut #88: Ctrl + Shift + #

Ctrl + Shift + # will change the date into a day-month-year format.

Shortcut #89: Ctrl + A

This is an alternative to Shortcut #13: Ctrl + Shift + Spacebar. Pressing these keys will also select the whole worksheet.

Shortcut #90: Ctrl + C

Ctrl + C will copy the contents of the active cell.

Shortcut #91: Ctrl + F

If you need to search for a specific data, you don't have to go to the Home tab and choose Find & Select. By pressing Ctrl + F, you can now access the Find and Replace dialog box immediately.

Shortcut #92: Ctrl + K

To insert or edit a hyperlink, use this shortcut.

Shortcut #93: Ctrl + R

This activates the Fill Right command. To use this, simply click on a cell you want filled then press Ctrl + R. It will copy all the formatting and contents of the cell to its left.

Shortcut #94: Ctrl + S

Ctrl + S will automatically save your file in its current name, location and format.

Shortcut #95: Ctrl + V

After doing Shortcut #90: Ctrl + C, you then proceed with Ctrl + V to paste the contents that you have copied.

Shortcut #96: Ctrl + Alt + V

Since the above shortcut will paste all the data as is, the Ctrl + Alt + V will give you most pasting options as it will open the Paste Special dialog box.

Shortcut #97: Ctrl + W

This combination is an alternative to Shortcut #66: Ctrl + F4, which closes the Excel program.

Shortcut #98: Ctrl + X

This will cut the contents of an active cell. When you say "cut", it will remove the data in a cell and will place it temporarily in the Clipboard so that you can paste the contents in another cell.

Shortcut #99: Ctrl + Y

The Ctrl + Y shortcut runs the Redo function, which means that it will repeat the previous command that you have done.

Shortcut #100: Ctrl + Z

Lastly, Ctrl + Z serve as the shortcut for the Undo function. This will reverse your latest command in Excel.

And that finishes our countdown for the Top 100 keyboard shortcuts in Microsoft Excel. To wrap things up, the last chapter will provide some pointers in "memorizing" these shortcuts the easiest way.

Chapter 6: Pointers for the Excel Novice

Most people will most likely feel daunted with the mere volume of shortcuts in this book. "How can I ever memorize a hundred of these combinations?", says most people. This fear of memorization only impedes the learning process. As such, you should stay away from this negative thinking.

Practice a Couple of Shortcuts Every Week

To be able to remember these shortcuts effectively, you should use them as often as you could. Have this book by your side always so that you will have a guide as you try to absorb each of these shortcuts. Better yet, you can jot down a couple of shortcuts in a small list so that you can try some of these tricks in your school or the office.

After finishing let's say at least five shortcuts for a week, add another five in the succeeding weeks. Just don't forget the previous shortcuts that you have learned. In no time, you will be able to use these keyboard combinations without the help of a cheat sheet.

Don't Use the Numeric Keypad

Although most people on the go use laptops such as students, many people still use the full-sized keyboard that has a built-in numeric keypad at the right side.

Although several characters in the listed shortcuts are there, the Microsoft Excel does not recognize the use of numeric keypad in its shortcuts. As such, you shouldn't try to practice these shortcuts via the numeric keypad; just use the main keyboard itself.

That ends all the pointers in this guide for Excel shortcuts. With that, you should apply all the learnings that you have discovered through this book in your daily Excel tasks. Hopefully, you'll be a more efficient Excel user as you incorporate these shortcuts in using the said spreadsheet program.

Conclusion

Thank you again for purchasing this book!

I hope this book was able to help you to learn the secrets behind mastering Microsoft Excel, which are the 100 keyboard shortcuts.

The next step is to make use of these shortcuts every time you operate on the Excel application. Through this, you can now easily work on your Excel spreadsheets with only a minimal use of a mouse.

Finally, if you enjoyed this book, please take the time to share your thoughts and post a review on Amazon. We do our best to reach out to readers and provide the best value we can. Your positive review will help us achieve that. It'd be greatly appreciated!

Thank you and good luck!

Book 2
CSS Programming Professional Made Easy

BY SAM KEY

Expert CSS Programming Language Success in a Day for any Computer User!

Programming Box Set #73: Excel Shortcuts & CSS Programming Professional Made Easy

Table of Contents

Introduction

I want to thank you and congratulate you for purchasing the book, "Professional CSS Programming Made Easy: Expert CSS Programming Language Success In A Day for any Computer User!".

This book contains proven steps and strategies on how to effectively apply CSS style rules in making your webpages more appealing to your readers. In this book, the different aspects of CSS programming are discussed in simple language to make it easy for you to understand even if you have no previous experience in programming. In no time, you can start creating your own CSS style rules!

Thanks again for purchasing this book, I hope you enjoy it!

Chapter 1: What is CSS?

CSS is short for Cascading Style Sheets which is a simple design language that is meant to streamline the enhancement of web page presentations. Basically, through CSS, you will be able to manage how a web page looks and feels. When you use CSS, you will be able to control the background color or image in the web page, the color of the texts, the style of the font, the size of the columns, the column layout, the spacing in between paragraphs and a whole lot more of design effects.

Even though CSS is quite simple to understand, it can provide you with great control of how an HTML document is presented. People who study CSS often study other markup languages such as XHTML or HTML.

What are the advantages of CSS?

- CSS will allow you to save time. After you have written a CSS code once, you can then use the same sheet in various web pages. You can create a style for each web page element and then use it to as many HTML pages as you desire in the future.
- Your web pages will load faster. If you will use CSS in your web pages, you no longer have to write an HTML tag attribute all the time. You simple create 1 CSS rule of a tag and then use it for all the incidences of that specific tag. When you use less HTML codes, it translates to faster download speed.
- Your web pages become easier to maintain. If you wish to create a global change in your website, all you need to do is adjust the style and then all the elements included in your different web pages will be automatically adjusted.
- You will be able to enjoy better styles compared to HTML. The style attributes available for HTML codes are lesser compared to what you can work with when you use CSS. This means that you will be able to create top quality styles for your web pages.

- You will have multiple device compatibility. With CSS, you will be allowed to use content that can be optimized for different types of device. Even when you use the same HTML document, you can present the website in various versions for different devices such as mobile phones, tablets, desktop and even printing.
- You will be able to adopt web standards that are recognized globally. More and more people are losing interest in using HTML attributes and have started to recommend the use of CSS.
- You get to future-proof. By using CSS in your web pages now, you can also ensure that they will have compatibility with future browsers.

Creation and Maintenance of CSS

Only a small group of people within the World Wide Web Consortium (W3C) referred to as the CSS Working Group is allowed to create and maintain CSS. This group generates the CSS specifications which are then submitted to the W3C members for discussion and ratification. Only ratified specifications are given the recommendation signal by the W3C. You need to note that they are referred to as recommendations since the W3C cannot really dictate how the language is to be actually implementation. The software the implement the CSS language is created by independent organizations and companies.

Note: If you wish to know, yes, the W3C is the group that provides the recommendations on how the Internet should work and how it should progress.

Different CSS Versions

The W3C released CSS1 or Cascading Style Sheets Level 1was released as a recommendation in 1996. The recommendation included a description of the CSS together with a basic visual formatting model that can be used for every HTML tag.

In May 1998, the W3C released the recommendation for CSS2 or Cascading Style Sheets Level 2 which included further information that builds on CSS1. CSS2 added support for style sheets for specific media such as aural devices, printers, element tables and positioning and downloadable fonts.

Chapter 2: Various Types of CSS Selectors

A CSS is composed of different style rules that are translated by the browser for them to be applied to the specific elements in your web page. A style rule is further composed of 3 parts: selector, property and value. A selector is the HTML tag wherein the style rule will be applied. Examples include <table> or <h1>. A property is the specific attribute type that an HTML tag has. In simple terms, you could say that each HTML attribute is ultimately translated to a CSS property. Examples of properties include border or color. Values, on the other hand, are directly assigned to the properties. For instance, for the color property, you can assign a value of #000000 or black.

One way to write a CSS Style Rule Syntax is: Selector (property: value)

Ex. You can write the syntax rule for a table border as: table (border: 2px solid #C00;). The selector in this example is table while the property is the border. The specific value given for the property is 2px solid #C00.

In this chapter, we will be talking about the different kinds of selectors.

Type Selector

The selector in the example given above (table) is categorized under the Type Selector. Another example of a type Selector is “level 1 heading” or “h1). We can write a CSS Style Rule Syntax as: h1 (color: #36CFFF;). The selector in this example is h1 while the property is the color. The specific value given for the property is #36CFFF.

Universal Selector

This is designated by an asterisk (*) which means that the style rule syntax that you want to create will be applied to all elements in your webpage and not only to specific elements.

Example: *(color: #FFFFFF;). This style rule means that you want all of the elements (including fonts, borders, etc.) in your webpage to be white.

Descendant Selector

You use the descendant selector when you wish to apply a certain style rule for a specific element that lies within a specific element.

Example: ul em (color:#FFFFFF;), the value #FFFFFF (white) will only be applied to the property (color) if the selector/property <em> lies within the selector <ul>.

Class Selector

Using the Class Selector, you will be able to define a specific style rule that can be applied based on the specific class attribute of elements. This means that all of the elements that have that specific class attributed will have the same formatting as specified in the style rule.

Example 1: .white (color: #FFFFFF;). Here the class attribute is "white" and it means that the color "white" will be applied to all of the elements given the class attribute "white" in your document.

Example 2: h1.white (color: #FFFFFF;). This style rule is more specific. The class attribute is still "white" and the style rule will be applied to the elements given the class attribute "white" but ONLY if they are ALSO an <h1> or "level 1 heading" element.

You can actually give one or more class selectors for each element. For example, you can give the class selectors "center" and "bold" to a paragraph <p> by writing it as <p class="center,bold">.

ID Selector

You use an ID selector to create a style rule that is based on the specific ID attribute of the element. This means that all of the elements that have that specific ID will have the same format as defined in the style rule.

Example 1: #white (color: #FFFFFF;). The ID assigned here is "white" and the style rule means that all elements with the "white" ID attribute will be rendered black in your document.

Example 2: h1#white (color: #FFFFFF;). This is more specific because it means that the style rule will only be applied to elements with the ID attribute "white" ONLY IF they are a level 1 heading element.

The ID selectors are ideally used as foundations for descendant selectors. Example: #white h3 (color: #FFFFFF;). The style rule dictates that all level 3 headings located in the different pages of your website will be displayed in white color ONLY IF those level 3 headings are within tags that have an ID attribute of "white".

Child Selector

The Child Selector is quite similar to the Descendant Selector except that they have different functionalities.

Example: body > p (color: #FFFFFF;). The style rule states that a paragraph will be rendered in white if it is a direct child of the <body> element. If the paragraph is within other elements such as <td> or <div>, the style rule will not apply to it.

Attribute Selector

You can apply specific styles to your webpage elements that have specific attributes.

Example: input(type="text"](color: #FFFFFF;).

One benefit of the above example is that the specified color in the style rule will only affect your desired text field and will not affect the <input type="submit"/>.

You need to keep the following rules in mind when using attribute selectors:

• p[lang]. All elements of the paragraph that has a "lang" attribute will be selected.

- p[lang="fr"]. All elements of the paragraph that has a "lang" attribute AND the value "fr" in the "lang" attribute will be selected. Note that the value should exactly be "fr".
- p[lang~="fr"]. All elements of the paragraph that has a "lang" attribute AND CONTAINS the value "fr" in the "lang" attribute will be selected.
- p[lang |="ne"]. All elements of the paragraph that has a "lang" attribute AND CONTAINS value that is EITHER exactly "en" or starts with "en-" in the "lang" attribute will be selected.

Multiple Style Rules

It is possible for you to create multiple style rules for one specific element. The style rules can be defined in such a way that different properties are combined into a single block and specific values are assigned to each property.

Example 1:

h1(color: #35C; font-weight: bold; letter-spacing: .5em; margin-bottom: 1em; text-transform: uppercase;)

You will note that the properties and their corresponding values are separated from other property/value pairs by using a semi-colon. You can opt to write the combine style rules as a single line similar to the example above or as multiple lines for better readability. The example below is just the same as Example 1:

Example 2:

h1 (

color: #35C;

font-weight: bold;

letter-spacing: .5em;

margin-bottom: 1em;

text-transform: uppercase;

)

How to Group Selectors

You can actually apply one single style to different selectors. All you really need to do is write all the selectors at the start of your style rule but make sure that they are separated by a comma. The examples above both pertain to the selector or property "level 1 heading". If you want to apply the same style rule to "level 2 heading" and "level 3 heading", you can include h2 and h3 in the first line, as follows:

Example:

```
h1, h2, h3 (

color: #35C;

font-weight: bold;

letter-spacing: .5em;

margin-bottom: 1em;

text-transform: uppercase;

)
```

Note that the sequence of the selector element is not relevant. You can write it as h3,h2,h1 and the style rule will exactly be the same. It means that the specified style rules will still be applied to all the elements of the selectors.

It is also possible to create a style rule that combines different class selectors.

Example:

```
#supplement, #footer, #content (

position: absolute;

left: 520px;

width: 210px;
```

)

Chapter 3: Methods of Associating Styles

There are actually 4 methods of associating styles within an HTML document – Embedded CSS, Inline CSS, External CSS and Imported CSS. But the two most frequently used are Inline CSS and External CSS.

Embedded CSS

This method uses the <style> element wherein the tags are positioned within the <head>...</head> tags. All elements that exist within your document will be affected by a rule that has been written using this syntax. The generic syntax is as follows:

```
<head>

<style type="text/css" media="...">

Style Rules

............

</style>

</head>
```

The following attributes that are connected to the <style> element are as follows:

- Type with value “text/css”. This attribute indicates the style sheet language as a content-type (MIME type). You need to note that this attribute is always required.
- Media with values as “screen”, “tty”, “tv”, “projection”, “handheld”, “print”, “braille”, “aural” or “all”. This attribute indicates what kind of device the webpage will bc shown. This attribute is only optional and it always has “all” as a default value.

Example:

```
<head>
<style type="text/css" media="screen">
h2(
color: #38C;
)
</style>
</head>
```

Inline CSS

This method uses the style attribute of a specific HTML element in defining the style rule. This means that the style rule will only be applied to the specific HTML element ONLY. The generic syntax is as follows: <element style=". . .style rules. . . .">

Only one attribute is connected to the <style> attribute and it is as follows:

- Style with value "style rules". The value that you will specify for the style attribute is basically a combination of various style declarations. You should use a semicolon to separate the different style declarations.

Example:

```
<h2 style ="color:#000;">. This is inline CSS </h2>
```

External CSS

This method uses the <link> element in defining the style rule. You can use it to add external style sheets within your webpage. The external style sheet that you will add will have a different text file that has the extension .css. All the style rules that you want to apply to your webpage elements will be added inside the external text file and then you can append the text file in any of your web pages by creating the <link> element. The general syntax that you will be using will be:

```
<head>
<link type="text/css" href=" . . ." media=" . . ." />
</head>
```

The following attributes that are connected with the <style> elements are as follows:

- Type with the value "text/css". This indicates that you are using a MIME type or a content type for your style sheet language. Note that you are always required to use this attribute.
- Href with value "URL". This attribute will indicate the specific style sheet file that contains your style rules. Again, you are also always required to use this attribute.
- Media with value "screen", "tty", "tv", "projection", "handheld", "print", "braille", "aural" or "all". This attribute indicates the specific media device that you will use to display the document. This attribute is only optional and it has a default value of "all".

Example wherein the style sheet file is named as docstyle.css:

```
h2, h3 (
color: #38C;
font-weight: bold;
letter-spacing: .5em;
margin-bottom: 2em;
text-transform: uppercase;
)
```

Then you can add your style sheet file "docstyle.css" in your webpage by adding these rules:

```
<head>
<link type="text/css" href="docstyle.css" media="all" />
</head>
```

Imported CSS

This method which uses the @import rule is the same as the <link> element because it is used to import an external style sheet file to your webpage. The generic syntax of this method is as follows:

<head>

<@import "URL";

</head>

Here is another alternative syntax that you can use:

<head>

<@import url ("URL");

</head>

Example:

<head>

@import "docstyle.css"'

</head>

How to Override CSS Style Rules

The following can override the style rules that you have created using the above four methods:

- An inline style sheet is given the number one priority. This means that an inline style sheet will always supersede a rule that has been written with a <style>...</style> tag or a rule that has been defined in an external stylesheet file.

- A rule that has been written with a <style>...</style> tag will always supersede a style rule that has been defined in an external stylesheet file.
- The rules that you define within an external stylesheet file is always given the lowest priority. This means that any rules defined within the external file will only be applied if the 2 rules above aren't valid.

How to Handle an Old Browser:

Currently, there are a lot of old browsers that are not yet capable of supporting CSS. When you are working with these kind of browsers, you need to write your embedded CSS within the HTML document. Here is an example on how you can embed CSS in an old browser:

```
<style type="text/css">

<!–

Body, td (

   Color: red;

)

-->

</style>
```

How to Add a CSS Comment

In case it is necessary for you to include an additional comment within the style sheet block, you can easily do this by writing your comment within /*....this is a comment in style sheet....*/. The /*....*/ method used in C++ and C programming languages can also be used in adding comments in a multi-line block.

Example:

```
/* This is an external style sheet file */
```

```
h3, h2, h1 (
color: #38C;
font-weight: bold;
letter-spacing: .5em;
margin-bottom: 2em;
text-transform: uppercase;
)
/* end of style rules. */
```

Chapter 4: Measurement Units

There are several measurements that CSS can support. These include absolute units like inch, centimeter, points, etc. They also include relative measures like em unit and percentage. These values are important when you want to specify the different measurements you want to include in your style rule. Example:

border="2px solid black".

Here are the most common measurements that you will use in creating CSS style rules:

Unit of Measure	Description	Example
%	Indicates measurements as a percentage in relation to another value which is normally an enclosing element	p {font-size: 12pt; line-height: 150%;}
cm	Indicates measurements in centimeter	div {margin-bottom: 1.5cm;}
em	A relative number used in measuring font height using em spaces. One em unit is equal to the size of a particular font. This means, if you want a certain font to have a size of 10pt, one "em" unit is equal to 10pt and 3em is equal to 30pt.	p {letter-spacing: 6em;}
ex	A number used to define a measurement in relation to the x-height of a font. The x-height is defined by the height of letter x in lowercase in any	p {font-size: 20pt: line-height: 2ex;}

	given font.	
in	Indicates measurements in inches	p {word-spacing: .12in;}
mm	Indicates measurements in millimeter	p {word-spacing: 12mm;}
pc	Indicates measurements in picas. One pica is equal to 12 points. This means that there are six picas in one inch.	p {font-size: 18pc;}
pt	Indicates measurements in points. One point is equal to 1/72 of one inch.	body {font-size: 20pt;}
px	Indicates measurements in screen pixel	p {padding: 32px;}

Chapter 5: Style Rules Using Colors

A color in CSS style rules is indicated by color values. Normally, the color values are used to define the color of either the background of an element or its foreground (that is, its text). You can also utilize colors to change how your borders and other aesthetic effects look.

Color values in CSS rules can be specified using the following formats:

- Hex code using the syntax #RRGGBB. Example: p {color: #FFFF00;}. The six digits represent one specific color wherein RR represents the value for red, GG the value for green and BB the value for blue. You can get the hexadecimal values of different colors from graphics software such as Jasc Paintshop Pro and Adobe Photoshop. You can also use the Advanced Paint Brush to get the hexadecimal values. You need to note that the six digits should always be preceded by the hash or pound sign (#).

- Short hex code using the syntax #RGB. Example: p {color: #7A6;}. This is the shorter version of the hexadecimal value. You can also get them from Jasc Paintshop Pro, Adobe Photoshop or Advanced Paint Brush.

- RGB % using the syntax rgb (rrr%, ggg%, bbb%). Example: p{color: rgb (40%, 50%, 40%);}. This format is actually advisable to use because not all browsers support this type of format.

- RGB Absolute using the syntax rgb (rrr,ggg, bbb). Example: p {color: rgb (255,0,0);}

- Keyword using the syntax black, aqua, etc. Example: p {color: red;}

Chapter 6: How to Set Backgrounds

What you will learn in this chapter includes how to define the background of the different elements in your web page. You can use any of the following background properties for specific elements in your webpage:

- You can use the background color property to define the background color of your element.
- You can use the background image property to define the background image of your element.
- You can use the background repeat property to control whether your background image will be repeated or not.
- You can use the background position property to control the position of the background image.
- You can use the background attachment property to define whether your image is fixed or will scroll with the rest of the webpage.
- You can use the background property to combine the above properties into one style rule.

Background Color

Here is a sample of how you can define the background color:

```
<p style=”background-color:red;”>
RED
</p>
```

This will result in RED.

Background Image

Here is a sample of how you can define the background image:

```
<table style="background-image:url (/images/pattern1.jpg);">

<tr><td>

The table now has an image in the background.

</td></tr>

</table>
```

How to Repeat a Background Image

In case your image is small, you can opt to repeat your background image. Otherwise, you can simple utilize the "no-repeat" value in the background-repeat property if you do not wish to have your background image repeated. This means that your image will only be displayed once. Note that "repeat value" is the default value in the background-repeat property.

Example:

```
<table style="background-image:url (/images/pattern2.jpg);

            background-repeat: repeat;">

<tr><td>

The background image in this table will be repeated several times.

</td></tr>

</table>
```

Here is a sample rule if you want the background image to be repeated vertically:

```
<table style="background-image:url (/images/pattern2.jpg);

            background-repeat: repeat-y;">

<tr><td>
```

The background image in this table will be repeated vertically.

</td></tr>

</table>

Here is a sample rule if you want the background image to be repeated horizontally:

<table style="background-image:url (/images/pattern2.jpg);

background-repeat: repeat-x;">

<tr><td>

The background image in this table will be repeated horizontally.

</td></tr>

</table>

How to Set the Position of the Background Image

Here is a sample of how you can define the position of a background image at 150 pixels from the left side:

<table style="background-image: url (/images/pattern2.jpg);

Background-position:150px;">

<tr><td>

The position of the background is now 150 pixels from the left side.

</td></tr>

</table>

Here is a sample of how you can define the position of a background image at 300 pixels from the top and 150 pixels from the left side:

<table style="background-image: url (/images/pattern2.jpg);

Background-position:150px 300px;”>

<tr><td>

The position of the background is now 300 pixels from the top and 150 pixels from the left side.

</td></tr>

</table>

How to Define the Background Attachment

The background attachment indicates whether the background image that you have set is fixed in its place or scrolls when you move the webpage.

Here is an example on how to write a style rule with a background image that is fixed:

<p style=”background-image:url (/images/pattern2.jpg);

Background-attachment:fixed;”>

The paragraph now has a background image that is fixed.

</p>

Here is an example on how to write a style rule with a background image that scrolls with the webpage:

<p style=”background-image:url (/images/pattern2.jpg);

Background-attachment:scroll;”>

The paragraph now has a background image that scrolls with the webpage.

</p>

How to Use the Shorthand Property

You can actually utilize the background property in order to define all of the background properties all at the same time.

Example:

```
<p style=”background:url (/images/pattern2.jpg) repeat scroll;”>

The background image of this paragraph has a scroll and repeated properties.

</p>
```

Chapter 7: How to Set Font Properties

What you will learn in this chapter includes how to define the following font properties to a specific element in your webpage:

- You can use the font family property to adjust the face of your selected font.
- You can use the font style property to make your fonts either oblique or italic.
- You can use the font variant property to include the "small caps" effect in your fonts.
- You can use the font weight property to decrease or increase how light or bold your fonts are displayed.
- You can use the font size property to decrease or increase the sizes of your fonts.
- You can use the font property to define a combination of the font properties above.

How to Define the Font Family

Here is an example on how you can define the font family of a specific element. As value of the property, you can use any of the font family names available:

```
<p style="font-family:calibri,arial, serif;">

This message is displayed either in calibri, arial or the default serif font. It will depend on the existing fonts in your system.

</p>
```

How to Define the Font Style

Here is an example on how you can define the font style of a specific element. The values that you can use are oblique, italic or normal.

<p style=”font-style:oblique;”>

This message is displayed in oblique style.

</p>

How to Define the Font Variant

Here is an example on how you define the font variant of a specific element. The values that you can use are small-caps or normal.

<p style=”font-variant:normal;”>

This message is displayed in normal font variant.

</p>

How to Define the Font Weight

Here is an example on how you can define the font weight of a specific element. With this property, you will be able to define how bold you want your fonts to be. The values that you can use are bold, normal, lighter, bolder, 100, 200, 300, 400, 500, 600, 700, 800, and 900.

<p style=”font-weight:normal;”>

The font is displayed with normal font weight.

</p>

<p style=”font-weight:lighter;”>

The font is displayed with lighter font weight.

</p>

<p style=”font-weight:800;”>

The font is displayed with 800 font weight.

</p>

How to Define the Font Size

Here is an example on how you can define the font size of a specific element. With this property, you will be able to control the font sizes in your webpage. The values that you can use include small, medium, large, x-small, xx-small, xx-large, x-large, larger, smaller, size in % or size in pixels.

<p style="font-size:18px;">

The font is displayed with 18 pixels font size.

</p>

<p style="font-size:large;">

The font is displayed with large font size.

</p>

<p style="font-size:larger;">

The font is displayed with larger font size.

</p>

How to Define the Font Size Adjust

Here is an example on how you can define the font size adjust of a specific element. With this property, you will be able to adjust the x-height in order to make the legibility of your fonts better. The values that you can use include any number.

<p style="font-size-adjust:0.75;">

The font is displayed with 0.75 font size adjust value.

</p>

How to Define the Font Stretch

Here is an example on how you can define the font stretch of a specific element. With this property, you can allow the computer of your webpage readers to have a condensed or expanded version of the font you have defined in your elements. The values that you can use include normal, narrower, wider, condensed, extra-condensed, semi-condensed, ultra-condensed, semi-expanded, ultra-expanded, expanded and extra-expanded

<p style="font-stretch:ultra-condensed;">

If this does not seem to work, it is probably that the computer you are using does not have an expanded or condensed version of the font that was used.

</p>

How to Use the Shorthand Property

You can utilize the font property to define the font properties all at the same time.

Example:

<p style="font:oblique normal bolder 20px calibri;">

This applies all of the defined properties on the text all at the same time.

</p>

Conclusion

Thank you again for purchasing this book!

I hope this book was able to help you to understand the basic CSS styling rules.

The next step is to apply what you have just learned in your own webpage.

Finally, if you enjoyed this book, please take the time to share your thoughts and post a review on Amazon. We do our best to reach out to readers and provide the best value we can. Your positive review will help us achieve that. It'd be greatly appreciated!

Thank you and good luck!

Check Out My Other Books

Below you'll find some of my other popular books that are popular on Amazon and Kindle as well. Simply click on the links below to check them out. Alternatively, you can visit my author page on Amazon to see other work done by me.

Android Programming in a Day

Python Programming in a Day

C Programming Success in a Day

C Programming Professional Made Easy

JavaScript Programming Made Easy

PHP Programming Professional Made Easy

C ++ Programming Success in a Day

Windows 8 Tips for Beginners

HTML Professional Programming Made

Programming Box Set #73: Excel Shortcuts & CSS Programming Professional Made Easy

If the links do not work, for whatever reason, you can simply search for these titles on the Amazon website to find them.

www.ingramcontent.com/pod-product-compliance
Lightning Source LLC
Chambersburg PA
CBHW052149070326
40689CB00050B/2826
9781518612503